Playing with Plays™
Presents

Beofrankula! A Monster Mash-up

A play in 3 Acts
Creatively modified by
Brendan P. Kelso, Angela M. Herrick, and Amanda Thayer

Ensemble cast size:
Minimum of 12 actors flexible up to 59!

Table Of Contents

Copyright 3

Director's Notes 4

Setting the Stage 5

Prop List..6

Cast of Characters 8

Opening 13

Beowulf..15

Frankenstein...40

Dracula 72

About the Authors 104

This play is dedicated to all the teachers
who love bringing the classic monsters to life!

Special thanks to Ellen Spondike
for inspiring this ensemble to happen!

Playing with Plays™ – Beofrankula! A Monster Mash-up

Copyright © 2004-2024 by Brendan P. Kelso. All rights reserved. Used with permission by Playing with Plays LLC

No part of this book may be reproduced in any form or by any electronic or mechanical means, including photocopying, recording, information storage or retrieval systems now known or to be invented, without permission in writing from the publisher, except by a reviewer, who may quote brief passages in a review, written for inclusion within a periodical. Any members of education institutions wishing to photocopy part or all of the work for classroom use, or publishers who would like to obtain permission to include the work in an anthology, should send their inquiries to the publisher. We monitor the internet for cases of piracy and copyright infringement/violations. We will pursue all cases within the full extent of the law.

CAUTION: Professionals and amateurs are hereby warned that all plays published by Playing With Plays may be produced only pursuant to a signed written license and are subject to payment of a royalty. The plays are fully protected under the copyright laws of the United States, Canada, the United Kingdom, and all other countries of the Berne Union,. All rights, including dramatic (both amateur and professional), motion picture, radio, television, recitation, public reading, internet, and any method of photographic reproduction are strictly reserved.

Whenever a Playing With Plays play is performed, the following must be included on all programs, printing and advertising for the play: © 2004-2024 by Brendan P. Kelso. All rights reserved. Performed under license from, Playing with Plays LLC, www.PlayingWithPlays.com.

For performance rights please contact:

contact@PlayingWithPlays.com

Viking illustration by:
Illustration 41201495 | Silhouette © Vadimmmus | Dreamstime.com

www.PlayingWithPlays.com

Printed in the United States of America

ISBN:
978-1-954571-27-3

Director's Note

Congratulations! You have been given a rare gift of infusing the love of classic literature into the minds and hearts of your actors and audience.

I originally wrote just Shakespeare and classics for Kids. Over time I learned that teenagers, and adults alike, were combining multiple plays creating longer performances. From this, my full-length plays were born.

The entire point of this play, and all of my plays, is to inspire the love of classic literature into the actors and audience. It is your responsibility, as the director, to make sure you create an environment for this to occur. Creativity is key to melodrama. By creating an open, energetic, and engaging environment, two things happen:

1) The artists care more about the end product and making the show memorable and
2) a performance that the audience will never forget!

This being said, if any actor has a creative interpretation they want to try to help tell the story, then let them try it! That's the beauty of rehearsals, it allows us to continue to try new ideas until something sticks and makes us all laugh.

Lastly, any lines you see highlighted in grey throughout the play are ACTUAL classic text. So, please don't be TOO creative with these! Everything else is fair game!

With these notes, I bid you adieu, and most importantly, be creative and have fun!

Break some legs!

-Brendan P. Kelso

Setting the Stage

You are doing three 1-act plays in one show, set in three different countries and three different time periods. Knowing that, a common set has to be generic enough to work for all. I have always been a minimalist when it comes to sets, as I like the focus to be on the actors. I use black boxes and minimal props for all my shows. I will occasionally do a backdrop if the actors want it. But, this is entirely up to the director and actors on how elaborate and creative they want to be!

Prop List

Below is a very basic list of props you will need for this performance. It is in no way definitive, as you may be as creative or minimalistic as you like.

Optional basic prop list for each play:

BEOWULF:

- Grendal's arm (gruesome, yet fun!)
- Swords
- Mead cups
- Bib
- Super powerful special sword
- Bunch of stuff made of gold
- Sign that says, "50 years later"
- Half-burnt clothing for narrator

FRANKENSTEIN:

- Pitchforks
- Don't forget torches!
- Random body parts (must have hand)
- Sheet to cover monster
- Food
- Books for De Lacey kids
- Sign that says "2 months later"
- Mirror
- Papers
- Dish gloves
- Dead flowers

DRACULA:

- Crosses
- Cross necklaces
- Papers
- Suitcase
- Mirror
- Pointy teeth! 4 pair: Dracula and Brides
- Full duffel bag
- "Kids-Meal" from restaurant
- Cowboy hat
- Dracula cape
- Shawl
- Blankets
- Coffin
- Stakes (wood, not food!)
- Cracker (holy wafer)

CAST of CHARACTERS

STAGE: a Stage Manager who does NOT do people
NARRATOR: Narrates and tries to survive the show

Beowulf
12 - 17 Actors

Approx Run Time: 25 minutes

BEOWULF: A fierce, humble, warrior who (almost) never fails!

[1]**HROTHGAR:** King of the doomed Mead Hall

[2]**GRENDEL:** Moor Monster who attacks for 12 years

[2]**GRENDEL'S MOM:** Mom out for revenge

[2]**DRAGON:** Dragon that defeats Beowulf (spoiler alert!)

UNFERTH: Soldier of Hrothgar; super jealous of Beowulf

[1]**WIGLAF:** Honorable soldier that helps Beowulf defeat the dragon!

WEALHTHEOW: Queen; married to Hrothgar

[3]**GEAT SOLDIER 1:** Eaten by Grendel

GEAT SOLDIER 2: Attacked by Grendel's Mom

GEAT SOLDIER 3: With Beowulf; killed by Dragon

[3]**GEAT SOLDIER 4:** With Beowulf; usually causing mischief with Geat Soldier 3

[4]**DANE 1:** Eaten by Grendel

DANE 2: Eaten by Grendel's Mom

DANE 3: Member of Hrothgar's Kingdom

DANE 4: Member of Hrothgar's Kingdom

[4]**GEAT TOWNSPERSON:** Member of Beowulf's Kingdom

The same actors can play the following parts:

[1]HROTHGAR and WIGLAF
[2]GRENDEL, GRENDEL'S MOM and DRAGON
[3]GEAT SOLDIERS 1 & 4
[4]GEAT TOWNSPERSON and DANE 1

Extra actors can play various other Danes, soldiers, or townspeople who are consumed by monsters and dragons!

There's a simple pronunciation key for the names and some words throughout the play, located at the back of the book.

FRANKENSTEIN
12 - 20 Actors

Approx. Run Time: 27 minutes

VICTOR FRANKENSTEIN: Bright, young, medical student

[1]**DR WALDMAN:** Victor's professor

MONSTER: Victor's creation (no, his name is not Frankenstein!)

HENRY CLERVAL: Victor's best friend

[2]**MOM:** a mom

[3]**SISTER:** Mom's daughter

[4]**BROTHER:** Mom's son

[7]**ANGRY VILLAGERS 1, 2, & 3:** They don't like monsters, and carry torches and pitchforks

[6]**MR. DE LACEY:** old, kind, blind man

[2]**AGATHA DE LACEY:** De Lacey's daughter

[5]**FELIX DE LACEY:** De Lacey's son

[3]**LITTLE GIRL:** lousy swimmer, saved by Monster

[5]**DAD:** Dad of lousy swimmer; lousy dad

[4]**WILLIAM FRANKENSTEIN:** Victor's little brother

[6]**ALPHONSO FRANKENSTEIN:** Victor's dad

ELIZABETH LAVENZA: Victor's fiancee'

[7]**VILLAGERS 1, 2, & 3:** find Henry and Victor

[1]**JUDGE:** a judge

RANDOM VILLAGERS can be extras as needed

The same actors can play the following parts:
[1]DR WALDMAN and JUDGE
[2]MOM and AGATHA
[3]SISTER and LITTLE GIRL
[4]BROTHER and WILLIAM

[5]FELIX and DAD
[6]DE LACEY and ALPHONSO
[7]ANGRY VILLAGERS and VILLAGERS

DRACULA
12 - 20 Actors

Approx Run Time: 28 minutes

JONATHAN HARKER: a lawyer

[3]**TRAVELERS 1, 2, and 3:** people scared of Dracula

COUNT DRACULA: a powerful vampire

[3]**BRIDES 1, 2, and 3:** Dracula's vampire brides

[1]**CAPTAIN:** brave man

[2]**FIRST MATE:** Second in command, not so brave

[3]**SAILORS 1, 2, 3:** Crew of the ship Demeter

MINA: sweet, brave lady

LUCY: Mina's cousin

QUINCEY: Texas cowboy, loves Lucy

DR. JACK SEWARD: runs the mental hospital, loves Lucy

[2]**ARTHUR:** lawyer, loves Lucy

[1]**RENFIELD:** wacky patient of Jack's, loves animals not Lucy

VAN HELSING: doctor and vampire hunter

The same actors can play the following parts:

[1]CAPTAIN and RENFIELD

[2]FIRST MATE and ARTHUR

[3]TRAVELERS, BRIDES, and SAILORS

OPENING

(GRENDEL runs across stage, looking hungry, holding food utensils, wipes mouth looking at various audience members deciding if they will be a succulent meal)

GRENDEL: Hmmm… you look tasty. Ohhh… but YOU look delicious! That buttery skin… *(approaches; hears noise backstage)* Hmph! You're lucky I have to go! *(runs offstage; NARRATOR peaks onstage)*

NARRATOR: *(to audience)* Is he gone? Oh, goody. That one is quite famished! *(straightens clothes and steps forward to address audience)* Welcome to our marvelous night of melodramatic monster mashups! *(TOWNSFOLKS with torches and pitchforks run across stage screaming for Frankenstein monster)* Hey, careful with those pitchforks and torches, people!!! *(to audience)* As you can see, it's already chaos backstage. But, lucky for you, we've rehearsed this at least five times and nobody in the audience gets killed, or hurt, or even maimed… I think. I did miss a couple rehearsals.

(DRACULA enters)

DRACULA: Is it my turn? *(looks to audience)* Whose blood do I get to suck?!

NARRATOR: NO! No, no! First, we agreed, NO AUDIENCE feedings. And second, you're not on till the third act!

DRACULA: That's so long. I am soooo hungry!

NARRATOR: No!

DRACULA: Just a little snack? Please. *(points at audience member)* Look. This one's small. No one will miss them.

(STAGE MANAGER enters: Dracula)

STAGE: Hey Narrator, have you seen… *(notices audience - freezes in stage fright)* There are people.

NARRATOR: Yes. They're called an audience. They're here to see the show. They were even foolish enough to pay money.

STAGE: *(continues staring)* I don't do people.

NARRATOR: Right, that's why you're the stage manager.

STAGE: Backstage. My thing.

NARRATOR: Okey-dokey. Let's just get you backstage?

STAGE: Right. *(continues staring frozen)*

NARRATOR: Hey Drac, can you help this one backstage?

DRACULA: *(looking and licking lips)* I would LOVE to! *(helps STAGE offstage)* Hello. I would LOVE to show you something.

(STAGE and DRACULA walk offstage)

STAGE: *(while leaving)* What big teeth you have. *(once backstage, scream is heard)*

NARRATOR: Well, looks like Dracula got his pre-show snack. But, enough interruptions! On with the show! Please, imagine if you will, Scandinavia in the early sixth century. *(starts exiting)* Oh! And ah… little known fact: Beowulf is the longest surviving old English text in existence. Enjoy! *(exits)*

BEOWULF

ACT 1 SCENE 1

GRENDEL THE MURDERER

(enter HROTHGAR)

HROTHGAR: I am a great king! I need a Great Hall as great as I! It will be a mead-hall grander than men ever have heard of.

(DANES run on stage and mime building quickly; they exit)

HROTHGAR: Oh look! It is finished!

(DANES run on stage; bow to HROTHGAR)

DANES: Hurray for King Hrothgar!

HROTHGAR: I will name it Heorot.

DANES: Hurray for Heorot!

HROTHGAR: Now let's have a giant party every night and be super loud to celebrate.

DANES: Hurray for a loud party!

(HROTHGAR and DANES start to dance, laugh, and party; enter GRENDEL)

GRENDEL: *(covering his ears)* Arrrghhh! What is this terrible joyful noise! Every night there is merriment and light-hearted laughter loud in the building! I am madly envious of the Danes' joy. *(uncovers ears)* The only way to stop it is to eat the people. *(to audience)* Yes! I'm a horrible monster who LOVES to eat people!

(GRENDEL tip-toes over to the party; HROTHGAR claps his hands to get everyone's attention; GRENDEL hides behind his own hands)

HROTHGAR: Well, I am off to bed! You all can sleep in this Mead Hall. I assure you it is safe and definitely, nothing bad will happen.

(exit HROTHGAR)

GRENDEL: *(turns to audience)* Ha, ha, ha, ha! He does not expect a thing!

(GRENDEL turns back to the "mead hall" where everyone is now laying down asleep; he knocks on the door)

DANE 1: *(answers the door)* Who's there?

GRENDEL: Rawwrr!!! I am the monster of evil, greedy and cruel, by the name of Grendel! Prepare to be eaten! Nom, nom, nom. . .

(GRENDEL eats DANE 1 at the door; DANES scream; GRENDEL chases some more people as DANES exit; he turns to audience, pulls out a napkin, and dabs at the corners of his mouth)

GRENDEL: Delicious humans! Mmmmmm . . . *(he approaches audience as if still hungry)* You look tasty. . . but we need the audience. . . for now. . . *(he gives audience a thumbs up before running offstage)*

(ALL exit)

ACT 1 SCENE 2

HROTHGAR and BEOWULF

(enter HROTHGAR and DANES)

HROTHGAR: *(wailing)* What have I done?! I have created a great hall and have put my people in danger! Hopefully, this monster will not come back again!

(exit HROTHGAR; enter GRENDEL)

GRENDEL: *(whistling; addresses audience)* Off to eat some more people! *(knocks at door, someone answers)* Rawwrr!!! I am the monster of evil, greedy and cruel, by the name of Grendel! Prepare to be eaten. . . again!

(GRENDEL eats some more people, wipes his mouth with a napkin, and runs off stage; enter HROTHGAR)

HROTHGAR: Noooooo! The monster has come back and will probably keep coming back for 12 years before someone comes to help us!

(HROTHGAR and his DANES wail loudly; DANE 2 crosses the stage with a sign that says "12 Years Later"; enter BEOWULF, GEAT SOLDIERS, and UNFERTH)

BEOWULF: I, the great and mighty Beowulf, warrior and champion of the Geats, servant to King Hygelac, have heard of your sorrows and have come to help!

(ALL stop crying)

HROTHGAR: How did you hear of our sorrows?

BEOWULF: *(leaning close to HROTHGAR, whispers)* Dude, you have been crying super loud for like 12 years, and I'm right offstage over there.

HROTHGAR: *(embarrassed, wipes face)* Oh right. *(cough)* Yes. Thank you for coming to our aid!

BEOWULF: I, the great Beowulf, alone now with Grendel I shall manage the matter, with the monster of evil.

HROTHGAR: Whew, that's a relief! I have been trying to figure out how to defeat Grendel for years and have failed. He's stopped by 4,380 times to feast on us!

BEOWULF: I never fail! I have defeated many a monster in my day! Including a sea monster. . . which is extra cool.

UNFERTH: Boooooo. That sea monster wasn't even that big!

BEOWULF: Who are you? And YES IT WAS!

UNFERTH: I am Unferth, great warrior for Hrothgar.

BEOWULF: *(to audience)* Obviously not THAT great. *(to UNFERTH)* You are just jealous of my greatness!

UNFERTH: Am not!

BEOWULF: Are too! And I heard you killed your brothers!

UNFERTH: Wow, that's a low blow… but… uhhhhh. … okay fine. I'll hang out right over here…

HROTHGAR: ANYWAY, back to me and MY problems.

BEOWULF: Right. Only with hand-grip the foe I must grapple, fight for my life then. If he win in the struggle, to eat in the war-hall earls of the geat-folk, boldly to swallow them.

GEAT SOLDIER 1: Wait. . . what was that?

BEOWULF: Sorry, quoting old text there. . . I am going to fight Grendel with my bare hands. If I win, he dies. If I lose, he gets to eat all of us, including you!

GEAT SOLDIER 1: Just to be clear, you're not even going to use a sword to fight a monster twice your size and there is a chance I might be eaten?

BEOWULF: Correct. *(smacks soldier on back)* You are a smart one!

GEAT SOLDIER 1: Great. Sounds like fun. *(to audience)* This is NOT what I signed up for.

HROTHGAR: Alright, let's get this party started!

(ALL cheer and exit)

ACT 1 SCENE 3

GRENDEL and BEOWULF

(enter DANES and GEAT SOLDIERS; ALL lay down to sleep; enter BEOWULF)

BEOWULF: Alas, everyone is asleep, but I am being sneaky-sneaky and only PRETENDING to be asleep to trick Grendel.

(enter GRENDEL this time wearing a crab bib; knocks on the door; GEAT SOLDIER 1 opens the door)

GRENDEL: Rawwrr!!! I am the monster…

GEAT SOLDIER 1: *(interrupting GRENDEL)* Yeah, yeah, we know… *(mocking GRENDEL)* "monster of evil, greedy and cruel, by the name of Grendel", blah, blah, blah…just get it over with.

(GRENDEL eats GEAT SOLDIER 1)

GEAT SOLDIER 1: *(to audience)* Yep. I knew this would happen. *(GEAT SOLDIER 1 dies)*

GRENDEL: Oooh! This one looks especially tasty! Time for a treat!

(GRENDEL walks toward BEOWULF; BEOWULF jumps up)

BEOWULF: Surprise! I am not asleep. Prepare to be defeated!

(GRENDEL screams; fight ensues)

GRENDEL: You will never defeat me! Ha ha ha! I am Grendel, the monster. . .

BEOWULF: Yeah, Yeah… we heard you. Let's just arm wrestle and settle this once and for all! *(to audience)* Little does he know that I am famous for my hand-strength.

GRENDEL: Fine! I'll teach you not to respect me!

(BEOWULF and GRENDEL arm wrestle; BEOWULF rips GRENDEL's arm off)

GRENDEL: Arrghh! You ripped my arm off! Not cool, man. I am defeated!

(GRENDEL grabs shoulder and runs off stage screaming; enter DANES, UNFERTH, WEALHTHEOW, and HROTHGAR)

DANES: *(start chanting)* Beowulf! Beowulf! Beowulf!

HROTHGAR: Woo-hoo! You did it! Now, Beowulf dear, most excellent hero, no lack shall befall thee of earth-joys any I ever can give thee.

BEOWULF: What?

WEALHTHEOW: He said he will give you whatever you want!

HROTHGAR: Yes, my beautiful queen is right, whatever you want!

(BEOWULF feigns bashfulness)

BEOWULF: Oh, I don't need much. I'm just glad I could help.

UNFERTH: Booooo! He wants treasures! He ALWAYS wants treasures! *(sarcastically mimicking Beowulf)* "Look at me, I'm Beowulf, I like LOTS of treasures!"

HROTHGAR: Unferth! You have nothing more to say, for Beowulf's actions speak louder than words.

UNFERTH: Sorry, king. *(quickly exits)*

WEALHTHEOW: My lord and protector, treasure-bestower, greet thou the Geatmen with gracious responses!

HROTHGAR: Treasure it is! *(turning to audience)* Got to do what the wife says. *(back to BEOWULF)* Here is a bunch of stuff made of gold!

BEOWULF: Awesome! Gold stuff!

(BEOWULF and GEAT SOLDIERS victory jump in the air)

HROTHGAR: Now let's have ANOTHER party! We can be as loud as we want since there is no monster to eat us!

BEOWULF: Let me just hang this arm on your wall. I think it adds a nice touch to the hall.

(BEOWULF hangs GRENDEL's arm on the wall; enter GEAT SOLDIER 1)

GEAT SOLDIER 1: Ew! Gross! Did you just hang Grendel's arm on the wall?

BEOWULF: Uhhhhh yeah. It's a battle trophy. Wait. . . aren't you that soldier that got eaten at the beginning of this scene?

GEAT SOLDIER 1: Oh yeah.

BEOWULF: Yeah.

GEAT SOLDIER 1: Yeah… soooo, this is awkward.

BEOWULF: *(motioning for SOLDIER to die)* Um, dude…

GEAT SOLDIER 1: Right! I'm dead…. Bummer.

(GEAT SOLDIER 1 falls over dead)

BEOWULF: Someone get this smelly corpse off the stage!

(ALL exit)

ACT 2 SCENE 1

THE MOTHER OF GRENDEL

(enter BEOWULF, DANES, and GEAT SOLDIERS)

BEOWULF: We have partied all night, let us sink then to slumber! You are all safe now, so I am going to go sleep in the castle. Bye!

ALL: Bye, Beowulf!

(DANES murmuring to each other as they go to bed)

DANE 3: What a great guy!

GEAT SOLDIER 3: I feel so safe with him around.

(DANES and GEAT SOLDIERS lay down to sleep in the Mead Hall; enter GRENDEL'S MOM)

GRENDEL'S MOM: *(to audience)* No one rips my son's arm off and gets away with it! I am on a mission, mindful of vengeance for the death of my son.

(GRENDEL'S MOM knocks on the door)

DANE 2: Who is it?

GRENDEL'S MOM: *(in high pitched innocent voice)* It's. . . uhhh. . . Aunt Judy. Oh, please let me in!

DANE 2: Aunt Judy! I was wondering where you went!

(DANE 2 opens the door)

DANE 2: Wait. You're not Aunt Judy.

GRENDEL'S MOM: Ha ha ha! I am Grendel's Mom! *(to audience)* Apparently, the author didn't have time to come up with a better name for me. *(to DANE 2)* Prepare to be eaten!

(GRENDEL'S MOM eats DANE 2; she runs around the Mead Hall roaring and eating people)

GRENDEL'S MOM: My son has been avenged!

(exit GRENDEL'S MOM; enter BEOWULF, stretching)

BEOWULF: Good morning, everyone! Where can a strong, humble warrior get a cup of coffee around here?

(GEAT SOLDIER 2 lying on the ground grabs BEOWULF'S ankle)

GEAT SOLDIER 2: My lord, we have been attacked. She goes by the name of Grendel's Mom.

BEOWULF: WHAT?! That's not very original.

GEAT SOLDIER 2: I know. But, that's her name. It's pretty lame. But, she was thirsting for revenge.

BEOWULF: Oh, and sorry you got partially eaten. *(steps over GEAT SOLDIER 2)* Fate has not been in my favor! I shall seek Grendel's Mother and avenge all of you!

GEAT SOLDIER 3: There seems to be a lot of avenging going on around here!

BEOWULF: It's part of our culture.

(enter HROTHGAR and UNFERTH)

HROTHGAR: What in the name of Fate happened here?!

BEOWULF: Grendel's Mom showed up to avenge Grendel. Now I must avenge your kingdom, AGAIN, and track down Grendel's Mom!

HROTHGAR: I'll come with you.

GEAT SOLDIER 3: Me too!

GEAT SOLDIER 4: Me three!

GEAT SOLDIER 2: Not me. I'm still wounded pretty badly over here. *(fake coughs)* You guys go on ahead. I think I'm just going to die. *(falls over dead)*

HROTHGAR: There are a bunch of us ready to go avenging now. Should we have a name for ourselves?

(ALL strike a thinking pose)

BEOWULF: I know! The Avengers!

UNFERTH: Boooooo. That's lame.

BEOWULF: Fine! You come up with something!

UNFERTH: Oh. . . uhhhh. . . I have to be somewhere. Bye.

(exit UNFERTH)

BEOWULF: He's your best warrior? Really?

HROTHGAR: *(shrugs)* When everyone gets eaten, you take what you can get. Anyway! We don't need a name. Let's go!

(ALL exit)

ACT 2 SCENE 2

BEOWULF SEEKS GRENDEL'S MOTHER

(enter HROTHGAR, BEOWULF, and GEAT SOLDIERS)

HROTHGAR: Here we are! The entrance to the monster's moor!

BEOWULF: All right! I'll just swim on down there and fight Grendel's Mom!

HROTHGAR: Whoa! You don't know how deep that water is! You should take soldiers with you.

(GEAT SOLDIERS whistle and look in opposite directions, hoping not to get chosen)

BEOWULF: Thank you, Hrothgar. But I will do this alone. If anyone helps, it will be way less impressive.

HROTHGAR: You are very brave. *(to audience)* Not too smart, but brave!

(enter UNFERTH)

UNFERTH: Booooooo.

(exit UNFERTH)

BEOWULF: My soldiers, if I fall in battle, send my high-valued jewels to King Hygelac. See you guys soon!

(BEOWULF "jumps" into the Moor; "swims" in place)

GEAT SOLDIER 3: *(to GEAT SOLDIER 4)* I can't believe he wants us to send King Hygelac his jewels if he dies.

GEAT SOLDIER 4: *(to GEAT SOLDIER 3)* Ugh, I know! We are the ones that helped him! Not King Hygelac!

(exit HROTHGAR and GEAT SOLDIERS; enter GRENDEL'S MOM)

GRENDEL'S MOM: Who is entering my lair? *(GRENDEL'S MOM sees BEOWULF)* You must be the one who killed my son!

BEOWULF: Yep. You must be the one who killed my new friends!

GRENDEL'S MOM: Yep.

(awkward pause)

GRENDEL'S MOM: Soooo… Should we fight to settle this?

BEOWULF: Sure. I'll just use this mysterious looking sword I found in your house.

GRENDEL'S MOM: That's fine, I guess. Prepare to be defeated and eaten, human!

(BEOWULF and GRENDEL'S MOM fight; BEOWULF kills GRENDEL'S MOM)

GRENDEL'S MOM: Really? Kill me with my own magical, super-powerful sword? Well, this stinks!

(GRENDEL'S MOM dies)

BEOWULF: *(to audience)* Ha! Two monsters in less than a week! I shall now swim back to the realms of day.

(BEOWULF "swims" back up; ALL exit)

ACT 2 SCENE 3

BEOWULF IS DOUBLE-CONQUEROR

(enter HROTHGAR and GEAT SOLDIERS)

HROTHGAR: Where could Beowulf be? It's been almost two days since he jumped in there!

GEAT SOLDIER 3: *(whispering to GEAT SOLDIER 4)* Probably dead.

GEAT SOLDIER 4: *(whispering to GEAT SOLDIER 3)* Let's divvy up his share of the treasures.

(enter BEOWULF)

HROTHGAR: You're alive!

GEAT SOLDIER 3: We thought you were dead!

GEAT SOLDIER 4: Good thing you're not! We definitely WEREN'T going to divvy up your treasure!

BEOWULF: Ohhhhkay. Anyway. . . I did it! I killed Grendel's Mom! I came off alive from this, narrowly 'scaping. Also, I saw Grendel's body down there and almost brought you his head, but I thought that might be too graphic for a kid's show.

HROTHGAR: Good call. The arm was kind of pushing it already, especially hanging it on the wall. Besides, it would be a lot of work to carry with labor the head of Grendel.

BEOWULF: Let's get out of here.

HROTHGAR: I have an idea! I know we NEVER do this, but we could probably have a party tonight to celebrate the defeat of Grendel's Mom!

GEAT SOLDIERS 3 & 4: Awesome!

(ALL exit)

ACT 2 SCENE 4

SORROW AT PARTING

(enter HROTHGAR, UNFERTH, and BEOWULF)

HROTHGAR: Well, he did it! Beowulf saved us and no one will ever be as good or as strong or as awesome as him in the whole world for the rest of time.

UNFERTH: Booooooooo. But good job, I guess. Here, take my sword as a gift.

BEOWULF: Cool! Thanks, man! Bros for life!

(BEOWULF and UNFERTH do a secret Bro handshake)

BEOWULF: Thank you, Hrothgar, for all of these cool presents and for letting me defeat your monsters. But now we must go home to seek our King Hygelac.

HROTHGAR: Can't you stay forever?!

BEOWULF: No. But if you ever need my help again, I'll be here. Just don't wait 12 years to tell me next time. *(ALL cheer)* Goodbye, friends!

ALL: Bye, Beowulf!

(DANES murmuring great things about BEOWULF as ALL exit)

ACT 3 SCENE 1

THE HOARD AND THE DRAGON

(someone walks across stage with a sign that says, "50 years later"; enter BEOWULF and GEAT SOLDIERS; enter GEAT TOWNSPERSON screaming and running across the stage)

GEAT TOWNSPERSON: A Dragon!! *(GEAT TOWNSPERSON exits)*

BEOWULF: What was that? Flagon?

GEAT TOWNSPERSON: *(runs back across stage)* A DRAGON!!! *(GEAT TOWNSPERSON exits again)*

GEAT SOLDIER 3: A what?

GEAT TOWNSPERSON: *(runs across stage again)* I swear I saw a dragon!! *(GEAT TOWNSPERSON exits yet again)*

GEAT SOLDIER 4: I think he saw a dragon.

BEOWULF: A dragon? Where? Not in my kingdom!

GEAT TOWNSPERSON: *(runs back on stage, hides behind BEOWULF, and peers his head around looking)* Yes! And the dragon is hoarding treasures! And breathing fire at the kingdom!

GEAT SOLDIERS 3 & 4: Treasures? Let's get it!

GEAT TOWNSPERSON: Go get the dragon? What?! *(faints)*

BEOWULF: No! My own native homestead, the best of buildings, are burning and melting! Treasures are nothing! I must defeat this dragon! For the safety of my people and also because I love fighting monsters.

GEAT SOLDIER 3: But, King Beowulf, you are like 70 years old now. You have been our King for 50 years.

BEOWULF: Don't worry. I'm still agile.

(BEOWULF stretches awkwardly to prove how agile and strong he still is; GEAT TOWNSPERSON and GEAT SOLDIERS nod, acting impressed)

BEOWULF: See? I've still got it! I feel no fear of the foeman's assaults and count for little the might of the dragon.

GEAT TOWNSPERSON: The dragon is literally destroying everything with fire and you don't think it is that strong?

BEOWULF: You got it!

GEAT SOLDIER 4: *(looking offstage)* Oh, and it has just started to eat people… ew… I think it just got the the narrator!

(NARRATOR runs across stage screaming with smoke billowing)

GEAT SOLDIER 4: Man, he is toast now! Ha! Toast! Get it? Because he was burnt?

GEAT SOLDIER 3: Just stop. *(shakes his head at audience)*

BEOWULF: Let's go slay us a dragon!

(ALL exit)

ACT 3 SCENE 2

BEOWULF SEEKS THE DRAGON

&

BEOWULF'S LAST BATTLE

(enter BEOWULF, GEAT SOLDIERS, and WIGLAF)

BEOWULF: Well, here we are! I braved in my youth-days battles unnumbered; still am I willing the struggle to look for. Who's with me?!

WIGLAF: We are, King!

(GEAT SOLDIERS all whistle and look in different directions)

BEOWULF: Ahhh...Thanks Wiglaf, my apparently one brave soldier, but your men need some help.

WIGLAF: Right... *(goes back to get his men in order)*

BEOWULF: Stay with your men, I got this! *(to audience)* More fun for me! Going at it alone like the good old days. I with prowess shall gain the gold or the battle! Wish me luck!

(BEOWULF charges forward; GEAT SOLDIERS all cower together at the side of the stage; enter DRAGON)

DRAGON: Who dares enter my lair?

BEOWULF: It is I! Beowulf! And this is MY lair!

DRAGON: Aren't you that 70-year-old king who did a bunch of cool things like 50 years ago?

BEOWULF: Uhhh...yes! But, I am still cool and now I am here to fight you!

DRAGON: Really? You do realize I am a dragon, right? I'm 6 times your size, breathe fire, have massive talons? Don't you want to send one of your younger, tougher soldiers to fight me?

BEOWULF: How dare you insult me! It is me and me only to measure my strength with the monster of malice. This is no work for a coward! Plus, I am still buff and strong. *(flexes)* So ha!

DRAGON: Alright then. Let's dance!

(BEOWULF and DRAGON begin to dance)

BEOWULF: Wait! I didn't come here to dance. Fight me!

DRAGON: Ughhhhh. Fine.

(BEOWULF and DRAGON fight; BEOWULF is hurt, falls and yells for help)

BEOWULF: Help! Help, my faithful soldiers!

(GEAT SOLDIERS run offstage)

WIGLAF: *(shouting after GEAT SOLDIERS)* Are you kidding me? Our King needs us!

GEAT SOLDIER 3: *(from offstage)* No way!

WIGLAF: We promised in the hall we would help Beowulf if need of such aid ever befall him.

GEAT SOLDIER 3: *(from offstage)* Blah, blah, blah. We get it! We made a vow. But, THERE IS A DRAGON OUT THERE!

WIGLAF: GET. OUT. HERE. NOW!!!

GEAT SOLDIER 3: *(GEAT SOLDIER 3 is shoved on by the other GEAT SOLDIERS)* Fine!

(as GEAT SOLDIER 3 enters, DRAGON kills him)

GEAT SOLDIER 3: SEE!!! Ugh! *(falls over dead)*

WIGLAF: Cowards! I'll help him alone then!

(WIGLAF runs to BEOWULF; DRAGON strikes BEOWULF; WIGLAF fights dragon; BEOWULF stabs dragon)

DRAGON: I should have stuck to dancing!

(DRAGON dies; BEOWULF collapses to the ground)

WIGLAF: My king!

(BEOWULF falls and is dying)

BEOWULF: Thank you for coming to help me. You showed tremendous honor, Wiglaf.

WIGLAF: You're welcome.

BEOWULF: I must die now.

WIGLAF: No!

BEOWULF: I am dead.

WIGLAF: No! Come back to me! Don't leave me!

(WIGLAF reaches over and picks up BEOWULF's knife)

WIGLAF: O happy dagger, this is thy sheath.

(WIGLAF motions to stab himself; BEOWULF suddenly wakes up; gasping)

BEOWULF: No! That is the wrong play!

WIGLAF: Oh, right. Sorry.

(BEOWULF dies again; WIGLAF sobs melodramatically)

ACT 3 SCENE 3

WIGLAF'S SAD STORY

(enter GEAT SOLDIERS; WIGLAF sitting with the newly dead BEOWULF; dead DRAGON lying nearby)

WIGLAF: Someone needs to tell the kingdom that their king is dead.

GEAT SOLDIER 2: I'll do it! *(screams)* THE KING IS DEAD!!!

WIGLAF: Go to TOWN and tell them.

GEAT SOLDIER 2: Oh, right.

(exit GEAT SOLDIER 2)

WIGLAF: We have recovered the treasure, but Beowulf's part of the treasure of jewels was paid for with death.

GEAT SOLDIER 3: We feel bad. . . but there was a dragon!

(GEAT SOLDIER 4 elbows GEAT SOLDIER 3)

GEAT SOLDIER 3: I mean. . . sorry.

GEAT SOLDIER 4: Wait, didn't you die?

GEAT SOLDIER 3: Oh yeah. Ugh!

(GEAT SOLDIER 3 falls down, dead; enter GEAT SOLDIER 2)

GEAT SOLDIER 2: I have told the kingdom the news! With King Beowulf dead, the folk now expecteth a season of strife.

WIGLAF: Oh great. We must honor King Beowulf's last wishes. We need to build a super huge monument with jewels on it by the ocean for sailors to see.

GEAT SOLDIER 4: That's weirdly specific for a last wish.

WIGLAF: Yeah, well, that's what he wanted.

GEAT SOLDIER 4: What should we do with the dead dragon?

WIGLAF: Get it offstage.

GEAT SOLDIER 4: Alright. But it better not stink up the backstage area.

(GEAT SOLDIERS 2 and 4 remove DRAGON from stage; GEAT SOLDIERS reenter)

WIGLAF: Okay, let's wrap this up. The name of this play is Beowulf, and because he is dead I guess that means the story is now over.

GEAT SOLDIER 3: Thank goodness. I'm exhausted from pretending to help fight monsters. I think I died like three times!

(ALL stand around BEOWULF's body)

WIGLAF: Gentlest of men, most winning of manner, friendliest to folk-troops and fondest of honor. You were a cool dude, Beowulf. Strong. Brave. Even a little crazy to think, at your age, you could fight a dragon by yourself. Okay. Bye.

(WIGLAF and GEAT SOLDIERS exit; play ends with BEOWULF lying on the stage)

(NARRATOR enters wearing half-burnt clothing)

NARRATOR: I'm so glad Beowulf got that dragon! Did it burn any of you? *(looks around)* No? Of course not. Well then, let's move on to our next monster... *(sees dead BEOWULF)*

NARRATOR: Yo! Dead Beowulf. Come on. Get up. Show's over. You got to get in the next show!

BEOWULF: Oh, right. *(exits)*

NARRATOR: As I was saying, our next monster is one we all...

DRACULA: *(enters)* You called? Is it my time? *(notices specific audience member, stares seductively and starts moving towards audience member)*

NARRATOR: No. Again. Third act. Now get... What are you doing?

DRACULA: You see that neck there?

NARRATOR: What?

DRACULA: There. On that person. It's so... smoooooth.

NARRATOR: Huh? Yeah, I-I guess so. Sure.

DRACULA: Their veins are right under the surface.

NARRATOR: Their veins? *(realizing what is happening)* Wait a minute! N-n-no, no, no! I promised this audience that no one would die in this show. We are NOT repeating what happened the other night. *(pushes DRACULA back)*

DRACULA: Look how many there are. They won't miss one.

NARRATOR: NO! Now go!

DRACULA: Fine! But I'll be back! *(exits)*

NARRATOR: *(mocks DRACULA)* I'll be back! *(returns to address audience)* Boy, keeping you guys alive is a full-time job! Now, where were we? Oh, right! Our next tale! Mary Shelley's Frankenstein! *(starts to leave)* Oh, and a little-known fact: Mary Shelley was only twenty when Frankenstein was published! Twenty! I just hope to be out of my parent's house by then! Ok, enough about me. On with the show! And a change of clothing.

(ALL exit)

FRANKENSTEIN

ACT 1 SCENE 1

(enter WALDMAN and VICTOR)

WALDMAN: Victor! Come in! You look so tired.

VICTOR: I'm fine, Professor Waldman! I've been working on an experiment. There's so much to be done.

WALDMAN: You remind me of myself as a young student! So few of us are willing to give our right arms for science!

VICTOR: You have no idea! *(to audience)* I will solve the mysteries of creation! *(laughs madly)*

WALDMAN: Pardon me?

VICTOR: I said…ahhh… I need a vacation! Gotta go back to work. Excuse me! *(VICTOR exits)*

WALDMAN: Strange kid.

(WALDMAN exits; VICTOR pops back on stage and addresses audience)

VICTOR: He'd think I'm mad if I told him! I've figured out how to make dead things live again! *(laughs madly, exits and returns with arms and legs)* I've been through dozens of graves and hospitals. Finally, I have everything I need!

(exits, laughing madly)

ACT 1 SCENE 2

(MONSTER is laying under a sheet; VICTOR enters)

VICTOR: *(to audience)* I see by your eagerness that you expect to see how it's done. Ha! If I showed you, you'd be…SHOCKED! Time to become the world's first bodybuilder! *(VICTOR laughs madly as he raises the sheet to hide himself and MONSTER)* To bolt or not to bolt, THAT is the question! *(there's a clap of thunder, then VICTOR yanks away sheet)*

MONSTER: *(sits up in monster voice)* GRR!!! GRR!!!

VICTOR: It's alive! It's alive!! IT'S ALIVE!!!

MONSTER: You never said that in the book!

VICTOR: I know but, it's more fun to say…IT'S ALIVE!

MONSTER: *(MONSTER takes one step towards VICTOR)* GRR!!!

VICTOR: OK!!! AAGH!!! Monster! *(screams and runs to other side of stage)*

MONSTER: Now THAT'S what you said in the book! ARGHHH!!!

(VICTOR runs away screaming, MONSTER takes the sheet and wears it like a cloak, exits)

ACT 1 SCENE 3

(VICTOR enters cautiously, addresses audience)

VICTOR: Oh, I did NOT think that through, I have created a mon...

(enter HENRY unseen by VICTOR)

HENRY: My dear Frankenstein! *(scaring VICTOR who screams and faints)* Victor? I wanted to surprise you with a visit. Are you okay?

VICTOR: *(waking up)* Henry, is that you?

HENRY: How very ill you appear!

VICTOR: I've been very busy, and I haven't allowed myself sufficient rest.

HENRY: Your family sent me to make sure you're not losing your mind.

VICTOR: My family? How are they?

HENRY: Your father's well. Elizabeth sends her love. Your little brother William just turned twelve. They really miss you!

VICTOR: That's it! I'm done with school! I want to go home! *(faints)*

HENRY: *(goes to VICTOR)* Whoa! I'll take you home.

(ALL exit)

ACT 2 SCENE 1

(MOM, SISTER, and BROTHER enter with dishes and pitcher)

MOM: Time for bed.

SISTER: Aw Mom, I'm not tired!

BROTHER: What if there's a monster under my bed?

MOM: *(to SISTER)* Did you make up another scary story!? Who do you think you are, Mary Shelley? *(to BROTHER)* There's no such thing as monsters.

(MONSTER enters unseen by MOM and SISTER)

BROTHER: But what about the one?

MOM: *(turns and sees MONSTER)* I didn't know it was Halloween!

SISTER: It's not. *(turns and sees the monster)* AGH!!! MONSTER!!! *(screams)*

ALL: *(screaming at each other)* AGGHH!!!!!

(MONSTER runs to hide behind BROTHER)

BROTHER: HELP!! He's gonna eat me!

(MOM and SISTER grab BROTHER)

SISTER: Help! Villagers! *(exit running)*

MONSTER: *(shrugs, finds food, eats it)* YUMMM!!! *(drinks from a pitcher)* AH!! *(goes to fireplace and warms himself)* OOHHH!!!! *(curiously touches the fire, it burns!)* AGHH!!!! *(dances around, blowing on his fingers)* OW! OW! OW!

MOM: *(offstage)* Be careful! It might still be in there. It better not be eating my food!

(MONSTER finds a cloak, hides under it; MOM and ANGRY VILLAGERS enter with torches and pitchforks)

ANGRY VILLAGER 1: Don't worry, Mam', it's probably just a bear.

MOM: That's no bear! It's a MONSTER!!!

ANGRY VILLAGER 2: Sure lady… a monster. *(VILLAGERS giggle)* We'll scare off your "monster".

ANGRY VILLAGER 3: YEP! Nothing big critters hate more than torches and pitchforks!

(VILLAGER 1 gets close to MONSTER with his torch and yanks off cloak)

MONSTER: AGHH!!!

ANGRY VILLAGERS: AGHH!!! It's a MONSTER!!!

ANGRY VILLAGER 1: Wow! You weren't kidding!

MOM: I told you so!

ANGRY VILLAGER 2: It's so big…and UGLY! Let's get it out of here!

(ANGRY VILLAGERS start cornering MONSTER)

MONSTER: You. Want. Piece. Me?! *(spoken in broken English)*

MOM: Catch him you fools!

ANGRY VILLAGER 3: On my count, 1,2,3,…

ANGRY VILLAGERS & MOM: CHARGE!!!!

(ANGRY VILLAGERS and MOM chase MONSTER through the audience and then ALL exit)

ACT 2 SCENE 2

(DE LACEY and AGATHA enter; FELIX enters with books; MONSTER enters and spies on family from front of stage, hiding)

DE LACEY: Good stew, Agatha! Just like Mama used to make.

AGATHA: Thanks, Papa!

MONSTER: *(to audience)* MAMA? PAPA?

DE LACEY: I may be blind, but you don't fool me. I know you always feed me first. I worry you don't get enough to eat!

MONSTER: *(to audience)* EAT. *(makes eating motions)*

AGATHA: Papa, you always put us first. Now, it's our turn.

FELIX: She's right! We love you, Pop!

MONSTER: *(to audience)* FAMILY. LOVE. *(whimpers)*

FELIX: This is getting way too mushy! Let's read Ruins of Empires, it's about manly stuff!

AGATHA: Felix, I was enjoying Paradise Lost! We were just getting to the good part! Adam was lonely and his creator was going to make him a wife.

DE LACEY: I'd rather hear a good war story.

AGATHA: Okay, Papa.

FELIX: *(to AGATHA)* I promise I'll read your book tomorrow.

(FELIX tosses book towards MONSTER who grabs it; DE LACEY, FELIX, and AGATHA exit; MONSTER looks at book)

MONSTER: BOOK. ADAM. CREATOR. LONELY.

(exits clutching book)

ACT 2 SCENE 3

(SOMEONE walks by audience with a sign that says, "2 months later"; MONSTER enters)

MONSTER: So, I've been watching the De Laceys and I've learned to speak and read. I learned that everyone has a family…except me. I read about a man who wasn't born but created, like I was. Only Adam's creator cared for him. Wait! Did mine make me beautiful? *(looks in a mirror)* AGHH!!! Nope! I'm ugly, SCARY ugly! Couldn't he at least find a good-looking fireman or someone? I mean, where did he even find a green head? And you try getting a good night's sleep with bolts stuck in your neck! *(sigh)* Now I understand all the screaming. Someone would have to be blind to be my friend! Wait a minute…

(MONSTER exits)

ACT 2 SCENE 4

(enter DE LACEY; MONSTER enters, knocks)

DE LACEY: Come in!

MONSTER: Hello! I'm a tired traveler. Could I rest here a minute?

DE LACEY: Sure, but I am blind and unable to procure food for you!

MONSTER: Don't trouble yourself. What I really need is a friend. If I don't make friends soon, I might do something I'll regret, and be an outcast in the world forever and ever!

DE LACEY: Don't get so overly dramatic! I'll help you make friends.

MONSTER: Really!?

DE LACEY: I'll introduce you to my kids. *(listens)* I think I hear them coming now.

MONSTER: Uh, oh!

(FELIX and AGATHA enter)

AGATHA: AGH!! MONSTER!! *(faints)*

DE LACEY: Where?!

MONSTER: Not again!

FELIX: *(chasing MONSTER)* Get away from my dad! I'll get my pitchfork!

MONSTER: Again with the pitchforks!?

(ALL exit, MONSTER exits running)

ACT 3 SCENE 1

(MONSTER enters holding papers)

MONSTER: *(angry)* Cursed creator! Why did you form a monster so hideous even YOU turned from me!? Nobody likes me! So I declare war against the entire species! Especially against YOU *(reads paper)* Victor Frankenstein. That's right! I found your notes and I will find you!

(LITTLE GIRL enters and falls making a "splash" sound)

LITTLE GIRL: HELP! HELP! I can't swim! *(keeps saying, "splash, splash…gurgle, gurgle")*

MONSTER: *(to audience)* Oh no, that little girl is drowning! I must help her!

(MONSTER saves LITTLE GIRL)

LITTLE GIRL: You saved me! Thanks, Monster! You're really sweet.

(LITTLE GIRL hugs MONSTER; DAD enters with pitchfork)

DAD: Get away from my little girl, Monster! *(pokes MONSTER in the shoulder)*

MONSTER: OUCH!!! I was just trying to give her a hand!! *(starts to run then turns back)* You're welcome! *(DAD tries to poke MONSTER again)* EEK! I'm outta here! *(exits)*

DAD: A monster was drowning my daughter! Bring the torches!

LITTLE GIRL: But wait, Dad...

(ALL exit chasing MONSTER)

ACT 3 SCENE 2

(enter MONSTER holding his shoulder)

MONSTER: *(to audience)* Ow! I save a human and this is thanks I get, the miserable pain of a wound!? I need a nap! *(lays down)*

(WILLIAM enters, he doesn't see MONSTER sleeping, he starts fishing)

MONSTER: *(wakes up and sees WILLIAM)* What a cute little human! I wonder if society has taught him to hate ugly creatures, yet? Maybe I could seize the boy and educate him as my companion and friend!

(MONSTER approaches WILLIAM)

MONSTER: Hey.

WILLIAM: *(still fishing)* Hey.

MONSTER: Whatcha doing?

WILLIAM: Um… fishing. You're not from around… *(looks over at MONSTER; gasps)* You're a MONSTER! *(screams)* PAPA, HELP!!

MONSTER: *(covers WILLIAM's mouth)* SHHH!!! I do not intend to hurt you!

WILLIAM: *(struggling to get free)* You wish to eat me and tear me to pieces! Let me go, Monster! Let me go or I will tell my papa!

MONSTER: No, no, no… we're gonna be best friends… FOREVER!

WILLIAM: No way! You dare not keep me! My papa is Mr. Frankenstein…he'll beat you up!

MONSTER: Wait! Did you say… Frankenstein!? Any relation to Victor Frankenstein?

WILLIAM: Yeah, he's my brother!

MONSTER: *(to audience suddenly turning evil)* He, he, he… Well, isn't that a coincidence! *(to WILLIAM)* You belong then to my enemy!? You will be my first victim!

WILLIAM: Victim? Wait…what!? Oh, this isn't good. Hey, about that best friend thing…

MONSTER: Nope! Too late for that!

WILLIAM: Uh oh!

(MONSTER bops WILLIAM on the head, WILLIAM melodramatically dies)

ALPHONSO and ELIZABETH: *(offstage)* WILLIAM! WILLIAM!

MONSTER: Oh no! Not MORE dreadful humans!

(MONSTER exits running; ALPHONSO enters)

ALPHONSO: *(sees WILLIAM's body)* My son is dead!

(ELIZABETH enters)

ELIZABETH: *(gasps)* NOOOO!!!! *(sobs melodramatically)*

ALPHONSO: My poor William has been murdered!

ELIZABETH: Only a monster can do something like this!

ALPHONSO: I won't rest until the murderer is found!

WILLIAM: *(wakes up briefly)* Thanks, Dad!

ALPHONSO: No problem, Son! *(WILLIAM dies again)*

(ALL exit)

ACT 4 SCENE 1

(VICTOR enters)

VICTOR: *(to audience)* This is terrible! I know exactly who did it, but who's going to believe me!?

(ALPHONSO and ELIZABETH enter)

ALPHONSO: Son, who are you talking to?

VICTOR: The audience, Papa.

ELIZABETH: My dear Victor! You look ill!

VICTOR: I'm fine. I just need to take a long walk in the woods.

ALPHONSO: But, it's midnight?

VICTOR: Yeahhhhh… Bye! *(VICTOR quickly exits)*

ALPHONSO: Strange kid….

(ALPHONSO and ELIZABETH exit, VICTOR reappears)

VICTOR: *(yelling into the air)* Alright, Monster! Show yourself!

(MONSTER sneaks up behind VICTOR)

MONSTER: BOO!!!

VICTOR: AGH! Don't do that! Listen, I have a bone to pick with you! You killed my brother!! *(VICTOR starts hitting MONSTER but MONSTER isn't fazed)*

MONSTER: You tired, yet?

VICTOR: No! *(stops, panting)* Actually…yes.

MONSTER: Good, because I want something from you.

VICTOR: What?

MONSTER: You made me SO ugly that everyone calls me a monster and runs from me. Except that person *(points to random audience member)* who keeps calling me Frankenstein. *(points at VICTOR)* He's Frankenstein, not me! Got it?

VICTOR: Achmmm, You were saying…

MONSTER: Oh, yes…I'm alone because of you! THEREFORE, you will make me a bride!

VICTOR: Make you a WHAT?! Have you got a screw loose!? No way!

MONSTER: You gave me bolts, not screws!

VICTOR: Whatever.

MONSTER: If I cannot inspire love I will cause fear. *(does Frankenstein walk around stage)* Do what I ask or you'll be sorry!

VICTOR: Listen, if you're not careful, I'm going to change your mind! *(to audience)* Literally!

MONSTER: What I am asking is reasonable. I'll take her far away to the wilds of South America where they don't have torches or pitchforks!

VICTOR: Fine. Promise me you'll leave, and I'll deliver into your hands a female.

MONSTER: I swear! Now get to work! *(hums Bridal March and dances as he exits)*

VICTOR: What have I gotten myself into? I must have a screw loose!

MONSTER: *(pops head onstage)* BOLT! You have a BOLT loose!

VICTOR: Go away!

(MONSTER exits laughing; VICTOR exits opposite)

ACT 4 SCENE 2

(ALPHONSO and VICTOR enter)

ALPHONSO: Victor, I've been thinking, it's time you and Elizabeth tied the knot! I booked the church for next Saturday.

VICTOR: Whoa! Saturday?! Ahhh... I've got things to do.

ALPHONSO: Like what?

VICTOR: I don't know... going to second-hand stores? Washing my hair? Touring the English countryside... yeah...

ALPHONSO: But why?!

VICTOR: BECAUSE!!!!

ALPHONSO: Wow, someone's moody before the wedding! Okay, but I'm sending Henry with you to make sure you come back...um, I mean to keep you company! *(exits)*

VICTOR: Okay, Dad! *(to audience)* Great! How am I supposed to rob graves and hospitals with Henry around?!

(VICTOR exits)

ACT 4 SCENE 3

(Enter HENRY and VICTOR)

HENRY: This is great! I've never been to England! Are you having fun, Victor?

VICTOR: *(gloomily)* Yea.

HENRY: Hey, why so glum?

VICTOR: I'm just… bored.

HENRY: Well, we're both students, it might be interesting to visit the universities.

VICTOR: I know, let's go see another cemetery!

HENRY: You're kind of weird, man.

VICTOR: How about you go visit the universities on your own, and then we can meet at Perth in a few months.

HENRY: Okay, see you soon!

(HENRY and VICTOR exit)

ACT 4 SCENE 4

(VICTOR enters wearing dish gloves and wiping his hands)

VICTOR: Ugh! Last time my eyes were shut to the horror. So much could go wrong! What if they hate each other? She might wake up and say, "Whoa! Who's the ugly dude?!" Ohhh…what if they really like each other, they might raise a family of monsters to destroy mankind!? Oh, the pressure! I'm coming apart at the seams!

(MONSTER enters with dead flowers)

MONSTER: I am here for my bride. It looks like she's almost ready.

VICTOR: We need to have a frank discussion! The deal… is off! *(exits)*

MONSTER: *(calls after VICTOR)* WHAT?! WHY?! *(VICTOR throws arms and legs onstage)* What do you think you're doing!? NOOOO!!!!

VICTOR: *(enters)* I'm saving mankind!

MONSTER: You fix her right now! Don't you dare break your promise.

VICTOR: Never will I create another like yourself! Get out!

MONSTER: Fine! I go; but remember, I shall be with you on your wedding night. *(does Frankenstein walk and evil laugh as he exits)*

VICTOR: Villain! I'll get you!

(VICTOR throws arms and legs at MONSTER)

VICTOR: *(to audience)* So, he thinks he'll kill me on my wedding night. Bring it on, Monster! *(looks out window)* Aghhh... I must set sail to meet Henry tonight. *(looks at body parts)* And I should really get rid of this mess!

(VICTOR exits with body parts)

ACT 4 SCENE 5

(VICTOR is laying down on stage; VILLAGERS enter)

VICTOR: *(wakes up)* Where am I? Where's my boat?

VILLAGER 1: You wrecked it in the storm.

VILLAGER 2: As for the place, you will know that soon enough.

VILLAGER 3: But you won't be consulted as to where you stay, I promise you.

VICTOR: *(gets up)* What? Why are you guys talking in riddles? I thought the English had better manners!

VILLAGER 1: I don't know about the English, but it is the custom of the Irish to hate villains! Am I right?

VILLAGERS 2 and 3: YEAH!!!

VILLAGER 2: Tell us what you know about the man who was found murdered here last night!

VICTOR: That's easy. I know nothing!

VILLAGER 3: Save it for the judge!

(JUDGE enters)

JUDGE: That's me. What's going on?

VILLAGER 1: We found a man on the beach last night. We thought he had drowned.

VILLAGER 2: Yea, only his clothes weren't wet.

VILLAGER 3: Then we noticed the black mark of fingers on his neck. He was strangled, your honor!

JUDGE: *(to VICTOR)* What do you know about this?

VICTOR: Nothing, your honor!

JUDGE: Nothing, eh? Okay, show him the body. Let's see if THAT jogs his memory.

(VILLAGERS bring dead HENRY onstage)

VICTOR: NOOO!!! Henry, you're dead, too?! *(VICTOR faints)*

HENRY: Yep! *(dies again)*

VILLAGER 1: He's ill!

JUDGE: Take him to rest…in jail!

(ALL exit)

ACT 5 SCENE 1

(Enter VICTOR and ALPHONSO)

ALPHONSO: Victor, I've come to take you home.

VICTOR: Dad! I don't think the judge will let me go.

(Enter JUDGE)

JUDGE: Of course I will! I'm the one who wrote to your dad.

VICTOR: Really? You believe that I didn't kill Henry?

JUDGE: I was very suspicious, but we were able to determine that your friend died before you arrived. So, I am pretty sure you're just crazy. I think your dad needs to take you home.

ALPHONSO: Let's get out of here, son.

(ALL exit)

ACT 5 SCENE 2

(ALPHONSO and VICTOR enter)

ALPHONSO: No place like home, right? Victor? What's wrong?

VICTOR: Don't you see? William and Henry, they died by my hand! I am the cause of all of this!

ALPHONSO: Stop saying that! People will think you're mad.

VICTOR: *(madly)* I AM NOT MAD!!!

ALPHONSO: *(to audience)* He's definitely loony! *(to VICTOR)* You couldn't have killed them. You weren't there when they died!

(ELIZABETH enters)

ALPHONSO: Elizabeth. Hopefully, you can help your poor fiancé.

ELIZABETH: I'll try!

(ALPHONSO exits)

VICTOR: Oh, Elizabeth. It's so good to see you!

ELIZABETH: *(upset)* Is it?

VICTOR: Of course!

ELIZABETH: Vic, we need to talk. We've been engaged for years. I love you, but don't marry me out of some sense of honor. Are you in or out?

VICTOR: I love you, too! Let's get married!

ELIZABETH: Really?! Oh, Victor. I'm so excited!

VICTOR: Uh, I do have one secret, it's a dreadful one. Can I tell you the day after our wedding?

ELIZABETH: Sure! Why not tell me a deep, dark, dreadful secret after there is nothing I can do about it and I'm stuck with you forever!

VICTOR: You're the best.

(VICTOR and ELIZABETH high five and ELIZABETH exits)

MONSTER: *(from offstage)* Remember, I will be with you on your wedding night.

VICTOR: Yeah, yeah. I know. If you kill me I'll finally be at peace, but if I win then I'll be a free man!

(VICTOR exits)

ACT 5 SCENE 3

(ALPHONSO, ELIZABETH, and VICTOR enter)

ALPHONSO: What a great wedding! Now off you go! Enjoy your honeymoon!

ELIZABETH and VICTOR: Thanks, Dad!

ELIZABETH: *(to Victor)* Let's go to our lake cottage! Where we can be alone and safe and NOTHING could ever find us!

ALPHONSO: Have fun!

(ALPHONSO exits; VICTOR and ELIZABETH walk around the stage)

VICTOR: This has been the best day ever!

ELIZABETH: Uh huh.

VICTOR: You are sorrowful, my love.

ELIZABETH: No. I'm happy my dear Victor. I have a weird feeling it won't last but, I'm going to ignore it!

VICTOR: *(startled)* EEK! What was that?!

ELIZABETH: I didn't hear anything.

VICTOR: *(quickly points to the other side of stage)* Did you hear THAT?!

ELIZABETH: What is it you fear, Victor?

VICTOR: I think it's just these very dark and spooky woods.

ELIZABETH: Oh look, we're here!

VICTOR: Oh good! Let's go inside. All will be safe… *(to audience)* tomorrow… But, tonight is… monstrous!

(ELIZABETH and VICTOR stay on stage; VICTOR is pacing)

ACT 5 SCENE 4

VICTOR: Go to bed, my dear. We'll be fine in the morning.

ELIZABETH: Okay. I'm fine now, but if you say so! Good night!

VICTOR: Good night!

(VICTOR and ELIZABETH high five; ELIZABETH exits)

VICTOR: Alright, do your worst, Monster!

(ELIZABETH screams offstage, then enters and dies melodramatically and MONSTER follows)

MONSTER: DONE!

VICTOR: THIS is what you meant by I'll be with you on your wedding night!?!

MONSTER: You mean you JUST figured that out? I thought you were a doctor or something?

(VICTOR grabs a pitchfork and jabs it at MONSTER)

MONSTER: Seriously! Why do YOU have a pitchfork!? You're not even a farmer!

(VICTOR stabs at Monster again)

MONSTER: Missed me! I'm outta here! *(exits laughing evilly)*

VICTOR: You won't get away with this!!!

MONSTER: *(from offstage)* Just did!

(ALL exit)

ACT 5 SCENE 5

(VICTOR enters)

VICTOR: Nothing is so painful to the human mind as a great and sudden change.

(ALPHONSO enters)

ALPHONSO: Victor! What are you doing here? Aren't you supposed to be honeymooning?! *(starts dancing)*

VICTOR: Dad, I have some terrible news.

ALPHONSO: What? Where's Elizabeth?

(ELIZABETH enters and dies)

ALPHONSO: NOOO!!! She was like a daughter to me!

VICTOR: I'm so sorry!

ALPHONSO: My heart is broken! Oh! It's really broken! *(clutches his chest and dies)*

VICTOR: Seriously? Ah, man!!

(VICTOR starts to move ALPHONSO and looks at ELIZABETH)

VICTOR: *(calling offstage)* Can I get a hand? *(a hand is thrown onstage)* Really!?

VICTOR: *(kneels)* My dear family, I'm off to avenge your deaths. I swear I will pursue the demon who caused this misery, until he or I shall perish in mortal combat.

(MONSTER enters laughing fiendishly)

MONSTER: You miserable wretch! Did you think I would let you take a bride when you destroyed mine? If I have to be alone then so do you!

VICTOR: *(getting up)* Monster, I will hunt you! I put you together and I'll tear you apart!

MONSTER: Whatever! I'm headed to the ices of the north! You'll suffer, but the cold never bothered me anyway. Come on my enemy, we may one day wrestle for our lives, but many hard hours must you live through until then. *(exits laughing evilly)*

(VICTOR chases MONSTER offstage; ALL exit)

(enter NARRATOR)

NARRATOR: The ices of the north, brrrr… no, thank you!

(MONSTER enters)

MONSTER: What's wrong with the ices of the north?

NARRATOR: Ummm, I'm sorry, but aren't you supposed to be backstage prepping for the third act? Or on a sled headed somewhere cold?

MONSTER: I was. 'Till you started criticizing me.

NARRATOR: Criticize? Now, that's an ugly word. I would prefer… opinion. Yeah. And we're all entitled to those. Right? *(MONSTER approaches)* Right?!!! *(hides onstage)*

(BEOWULF enters)

BEOWULF: I can vanquish your monster for you!

NARRATOR: Yay!

MONSTER: Didn't you die in the first act?

BEOWULF: Oh, yeah. *(starts exiting)*

NARRATOR: No! No, no, no, don't leave! Vanquish! Vanquish away!

BEOWULF: Yes! I am the ghost of Beowulf, still strong enough to vanquish monsters!

(BEOWULF and MONSTER square off)

NARRATOR: *(to audience)* I can't believe I'm doing this. *(calls backstage)* Hey, Dracula!

(DRACULA enters; ALL stare as he approaches center; strikes a pose)

DRACULA: Yes?!

NARRATOR: You kept saying you were hungry? I got these two guys for you. Free!

(DRACULA looks them over)

DRACULA: But neither has blood. It's like you don't even know who I am anymore.

NARRATOR: Sorry.

DRACULA: *(to MONSTER)* I'm a little tired of this one. Would you mind getting rid of him for me?

MONSTER: I would LOVE to! *(approaches NARRATOR)*

NARRATOR: Noooo! *(runs offstage)*

MONSTER: *(to DRACULA)* When will they learn, running never helps. *(MONSTER follows offstage)*

DRACULA: I know. Right?

BEOWULF: The hunt is on! I feel so alive again! *(exits following)*

DRACULA: *(pauses to relish audience)* You. You look… delicious. What are you doing after the show? Perhaps you can come down to my chambers and have a little… midnight snack?

(STAGE enters; pale with two dots on her neck)

STAGE: *(yelling)* Intermission! *(sees DRACULA)*

DRACULA: Well… hello, again.

STAGE: Oh, no, no, no!!! *(exits)*

DRACULA: *(to audience)* I know what I'M having for intermission! See you in fifteen! *(exits)*

INTERMISSION

(enter NARRATOR)

NARRATOR: Hello, again! You know what's a bad idea? Having a hungry Dracula backstage for intermission. Bad, bad idea. We just lost half our cast and crew! I narrowly escaped, myself!

(DRACULA enters wiping mouth)

DRACULA: Did someone say my name?

(NARRATOR pulls out cross)

NARRATOR: Stay away!

DRACULA: Relax, relax. I'm full... for now.

NARRATOR: Well, that's good. Because it's finally time for your show.

DRACULA: Great! Now to see what a REAL monster can do. On with MY show! *(exits flourishing)*

NARRATOR: Man, is that guy full of himself, or what? Actually, come to think of it, he's full of everyone else, isn't he? Huh. Oh, well. *(starts to exit)* Oh! And a little fun fact. Bram Stoker, who wrote Dracula, never once went to Transylvania! And yes, it is a real place! Enjoy the show! *(exits)*

DRACULA

ACT 1 SCENE 1

(JONATHAN and TRAVELERS enter)

JONATHAN: Made it to Transylvania. Hello. Where do I catch the stagecoach to Borgo Pass?

(The TRAVELERS gasp; TRAVELER 2 crosses self; TRAVELERS 1 and 3 make a "V" sign with their index and middle fingers pointed at JONATHAN)

JONATHAN: Was it something I said?

TRAVELER 1: Why would you go there?

JONATHAN: I have business with Count Dracula.

(TRAVELERS repeat their reactions)

JONATHAN: What are you doing?!

TRAVELER 3: We guard against the evil eye!

JONATHAN: The what?!?

TRAVELER 2: *(hands cross necklace to JONATHAN)* Wear this!

JONATHAN: Why?

TRAVELER 2: For your mother's sake. *(sobs)*

JONATHAN: Oookay. *(puts on necklace)* There's my stagecoach. Gotta go! *(exits)*

TRAVELER 3: For the dead travel fast.

JONATHAN: *(re-enters)* What?

TRAVELERS: Nothing. *(JONATHAN exits)*

(TRAVELERS repeat their reactions; exit)

ACT 1 SCENE 2

(JONATHAN enters)

JONATHAN: That's one spooky castle. *(wolves howl)* Ahhhhh!

(JONATHAN "knocks"; DRACULA enters)

DRACULA: Welcome to my house. Come freely. Go safely, and leave something of the happiness you bring! I'm Dracula.

JONATHAN: I'm your new lawyer, Jonathan Harker, Mr. Hawkins sent me. *(shakes DRACULA's hand)* Wow, your hand is cold!

DRACULA: *(laughs)* Please come in. My servants made you dinner. I... dined earlier, but maybe I can make YOU dinner on another night.

JONATHAN: Thanks. *(hands DRACULA papers from his suitcase)* Here are the papers. Just sign there, and you'll be the new owner of Carfax Abbey in England.

(DRACULA signs, wolves howl)

DRACULA: Listen to them—the children of the night. What music they make!

JONATHAN: Yeah... Well, congratulations. I'll return to England in the morning, my fiance' Mina is waiting for me.

DRACULA: You must stay for a month to teach me English.

JONATHAN: Do you wish me to stay so long?

DRACULA: I'm moving to England, I want to sound like a true Englishman. Your boss Mr. Hawkins said you'd help me.

JONATHAN: Okay. I'll write to Mina and let her know.

DRACULA: You may go anywhere you wish in the castle, except where the doors are locked. There's a reason that all things are as they are. Dream well.

JONATHAN: Goodnight. *(DRACULA exits)* Weird dude.

(exits)

ACT 1 SCENE 3

(JONATHAN enters holding a mirror; "shaves")

JONATHAN: This castle doesn't have any mirrors. Good thing I brought my own.

(DRACULA enters behind JONATHAN)

DRACULA: Good evening.

JONATHAN: *(cuts himself)* Ow!

DRACULA: Did I scare you?

JONATHAN: No. You surprised me, I didn't see you in my mirror.

DRACULA: *(sees cut; tries to "bite" JONATHAN; sees cross necklace; stops)* Take care how you cut yourself. It is more dangerous than you think in this country. *(grabs mirror)*

JONATHAN: What are you doing?

DRACULA: This wretched thing has done the mischief. It's a foul bauble of man's vanity. Away with it! *(tosses mirror)*

JONATHAN: Hey!

DRACULA: Your dinner is ready. I must go.

JONATHAN: Aren't you going to eat first?

DRACULA: I'll pick up someone - errr something while I'm out. *(exits laughing evilly)*

JONATHAN: Later! *(to audience)* How strange! *(looks offstage)* What's that? Someone's crawling on the castle. It's Dracula! Whoa! He turned into a bat! I've gotta get out of here!

(exits)

ACT 1 SCENE 4

(JONATHAN enters)

JONATHAN: *(to audience)* Every door is locked. I can't escape! I'm exhausted. *(sleeps)*

(The BRIDES enter)

BRIDE 1: I'm hungry. Where's Dracula?

BRIDE 2: Yeah! I need a BITE.

BRIDE 3: Someone's sleeping on my couch! *(points at JONATHAN)*

BRIDE 1: He's cute!

BRIDE 2: Let's kiss him!

BRIDES 1 and 3: Ew!!!

BRIDE 2: Not a real kiss. We'll suck his blood.

BRIDE 3: Me first!

BRIDE 1: No, me!

(BRIDES 1 and 3 fight)

BRIDE 2: Stop! *(to BRIDE 3)* He's on your couch. Go on! You're first and we shall follow.

(BRIDE 3 wakes JONATHAN)

JONATHAN: You're pretty!

BRIDE 3: Kiss me.

JONATHAN: Really? Um, I can't, I'm engaged. *(Bride 3 opens her mouth; comes toward him)* Whoa! What pointy teeth you have!

BRIDE 3: The better to...

(DRACULA enters; pulls BRIDE 3 away from JONATHAN)

DRACULA: How dare you touch him! This man belongs to me.

BRIDE 2: But we're hungry!

DRACULA: When I am done with him you shall kiss him at your will.

JONATHAN: What?

BRIDE 1: Are we to have nothing to-night?

BRIDE 3: You said you'd bring home dinner.

DRACULA: Don't BITE the hand that feeds you! *(exits laughing; re-enters with duffle bag)* Here, I picked you up a KID meal.

BRIDES: Yay! *(grab bag and exit)*

DRACULA: Jonathan, go back to your bed. For your rest will then be safe.

JONATHAN: No, I want to go home!

DRACULA: You'll leave in the morning.

JONATHAN: Why may I not go to-night?

DRACULA: My coachman and horses are away. *(wolves howl)* And there's that.

JONATHAN: Fine. I shall wait till morning!

DRACULA: Smart choice. Goodnight!

(JONATHAN starts to exit; hides as BRIDES enter)

BRIDE 1: We're still hungry!

BRIDE 2: Yeah!

BRIDE 3: Why must we share when you get your own meal?

DRACULA: Have patience, my brides! To-night is mine. To-morrow is yours! The movers will pick up my coffins of Transylvanian soil at dawn. Once I'm off to prepare our home in England, you can make Jonathan a vampire.

BRIDE 1: Mmmm, new blood! Double, double toil, and trouble!

BRIDE 2: No, no, no... we're vampires, not witches!

BRIDE 3: Yeah. We say blah, blah, blah!

DRACULA: Aghhh! How many times do I tell you! We do NOT say blah, blah, blah! *(aside)* Vampire brides!

(VAMPIRES exit)

JONATHAN: *(to audience)* He's going to England, and they want to turn me into a vampire! I must escape!

(exits)

ACT 2 SCENE 1

(enter CAPTAIN wearing cross necklace, FIRST MATE, and SAILORS)

CAPTAIN: All fifty coffins are onboard. Time for the Demeter to sail for England.

SAILOR 3: Who's shipping all this dirt, Captain? And in coffins? Spooky!?

CAPTAIN: *(reads paper)* It's going to England on behalf of Count Dracula.

(SAILORS gasp; two make "V" sign; one crosses self)

FIRST MATE: Get to work! There's no time for silly superstitions.

(SAILORS exits)

CAPTAIN: Take it easy, First Mate. They're all steady fellows, who have sailed with me before. They're tired from lifting those coffins. That last one was DEAD weight.

(scream offstage, SAILORS 1 and 2 enter)

FIRST MATE: What was that?

SAILOR 1: Petrofsky screamed, Sir.

SAILOR 2: We can't find him.

SAILOR 1: I thought I saw him in the shadows, but it was a stranger with pointy teeth!

FIRST MATE: Nonsense! Back to work!

SAILORS: Yes, Sir. *(exit)*

CAPTAIN: The storm has them spooked.

FIRST MATE: When I find Petrofsky, I'll...

(SAILOR 1 screams, SAILOR 2 enters)

CAPTAIN: What happened?!

SAILOR 2: The others are dead below!

CAPTAIN: NO!!!

SAILOR 2: Yes!!! Captain, I'm scared!

FIRST MATE: You're not paid to be scared. Take a torch down there and find the trouble.

CAPTAIN: You should go, too.

FIRST MATE: What about you?

CAPTAIN: I have to steer the ship.

FIRST MATE: Fine!

(SAILOR 2 and FIRST MATE exit; FIRST MATE re-enters screaming)

CAPTAIN: What's wrong?

FIRST MATE: The crew is dead!

CAPTAIN: WHAT!?

(SAILORS enter and die melodramatically)

CAPTAIN: How did this happen?

FIRST MATE: HE is here! The sea will save me from HIM! You'd better come too, Captain!

CAPTAIN: I can't leave my ship.

FIRST MATE: You're batty! Later! *("jumps" in the water)* SPLASH!

CAPTAIN: I'M batty?!

(DRACULA enters)

CAPTAIN: Uh, oh! Good thing I'm wearing my cross necklace! I'm outta here! *(exits)*

DRACULA: Bummer, there goes dessert! *(exits)*

ACT 2 SCENE 2

(LUCY and MINA enter)

LUCY: Cousin Mina! I've missed you!

MINA: There are darknesses in life and there are lights, and you are one of the lights. I've missed you too, Lucy!

LUCY: I'm glad you made it through the crowd. They all want to see the ship that wrecked last night. It's only cargo was some boxes of dirt, and the crew was murdered! Weird!

MINA: That's a lot of excitement for a small town.

LUCY: There's more excitement tonight. We're having a party!

MINA: I don't feel like partying.

LUCY: Still worried about Jonathan?

MINA: I've not heard from Jonathan for some time. I'm very concerned.

LUCY: The party will distract you. *(QUINCEY and JACK enter)* Evening, gentlemen. Mina, this is Quincey, a cowboy from Texas.

QUINCEY: Howdy! *(tips hat)*

LUCY: This is Dr. Seward, he runs the lunatic asylum.

JACK: She means the Mental Hospital. Call me Jack.

LUCY: He's rich and clever, just right for you... if Jonathan doesn't return.

MINA: Lucy!

LUCY: I mean, you two should dance! *(pushes MINA and JACK to dance)*

QUINCEY: Miss Lucy, won't you just hitch up alongside me and go down the long road, driving in double harness?

LUCY: What? I don't know anything of hitching.

QUINCEY: Marry me?

LUCY: There's someone else.

QUINCEY: Then, I'll be your faithful friend. *(to MINA)* Wanna dance?

(QUINCEY and MINA dance; JACK crosses to LUCY)

JACK: Lucy, you're dear to me. PLEASE marry me.

(enter ARTHUR)

LUCY: I can't, I love Arthur.

ARTHUR: And I love Lucy! Marry me?

LUCY: Yes! *(high fives ARTHUR)* Mina, we have a wedding to plan!

(ALL exit)

ACT 2 SCENE 3

(JACK enters)

JACK: Lucy broke my heart. Guess I'll visit my favorite patient. *(RENFIELD enters)* Renfield's probably dangerous, definitely batty, but REALLY interesting!

RENFIELD: I'm the guy who swallowed some flies. I won't say why I swallowed those flies, then I went and swallowed some spiders that giggled and wiggled inside here *(points to tummy)*, and I'm sure that you've heard I swallowed some birds...

JACK: Yes, you've eaten every pet we've given you.

RENFIELD: Master says, "Blood is life."

JACK: What? Who is "Master"?

RENFIELD: You'll know soon enough.

JACK: Goodnight, Renfield.

RENFIELD: Wait, Doctor! Can I have a cat?

JACK: Go to bed, Renfield.

RENFIELD: Blood is life! *(exits)*

JACK: He's loony!

(exits)

ACT 3 SCENE 1

MINA: *(offstage)* Lucy, where are you? Are you sleepwalking outside AGAIN?

(LUCY enters sleepwalking; DRACULA follows)

LUCY: *(sees DRACULA)* You're handsome! Am I dreaming?

DRACULA: You are now! *(hypnotizes her)* You like me and want me to bite you.

LUCY: Okay.

DRACULA: Now, you're caught in a BAT romance! *(laughs evilly; puts his cape around LUCY and makes slurping noises)*

(MINA enters wearing a shawl)

MINA: Lucy? Lucy?! Are you in the garden? *(sees DRACULA)* Who are you? Get away from her! *(DRACULA exits)* Who was that?

LUCY: *(wakes)* I didn't see anyone.

MINA: Are you okay?

LUCY: I'm cold.

MINA: Here, take my warm shawl. Let's go home.

(MINA and LUCY exit)

ACT 3 SCENE 2

(LUCY sleeps, with two red dots on her neck; MINA enters)

MINA: Lucy, it's afternoon. Wake up! Are you alright?

LUCY: I'm DEAD tired.

MINA: You're pale. Do you have a fever? *(puts hand on LUCY's forehead, sees dots)* Oh no! You have two little wounds on your neck.

LUCY: I did not even feel it.

MINA: I woke you because I have news of Jonathan. The dear fellow has been ill; that is why he did not write. I'm going to Transylvania to bring him home. We are to be married out there. Lucy? Aren't you excited?

LUCY: I'm happy for you, but my throat pains me. It must be something wrong with my lungs, for I don't seem to get air enough.

MINA: I must go, but I'll send Jack to examine you. Goodbye, sweet Lucy! *(exits)*

ACT 3 SCENE 3

(JACK and VAN HELSING enter, LUCY sits)

JACK: Lucy, this is Doctor Van Helsing, who knows much about obscure diseases.

LUCY: Pleasure to meet you. And... cool name.

VAN HELSING: Thank you, young Miss. Let's see your neck. Hmmm. Take a deep breath. Good. Jack, come with me.

(they move downstage, LUCY sleeps)

JACK: What's wrong?

VAN HELSING: There must be a transfusion of blood, or she will die.

JACK: I am younger and stronger, Professor. It must be me.

(ARTHUR enters)

ARTHUR: What's going on? Lucy looks...drained.

VAN HELSING: Drained is right. She wants blood, and blood she must have or die!

ARTHUR: What can I do? Tell me, and I shall do it. My life is hers, and I would give the last drop of blood in my body for her.

VAN HELSING: We don't need THAT much. *(covers ARTHUR and LUCY's arms with a blanket)* Here we go.

JACK: All done, go rest.

ARTHUR: I'm fine. *(faints)*

(QUINCEY enters; steps over ARTHUR)

QUINCEY: I heard Lucy was sick. How can I help?

VAN HELSING: Roll up your sleeve. You too, Jack. She needs blood from all of us.

JACK: How did she lose so much? There's only a couple of drops on her pillow.

VAN HELSING: *(spookily)* The better question is: What took it out?

QUINCEY: Back home, we have giant Vampire bats that suck cow's blood. Y'all have those here?

VAN HELSING: We have something, or should I say SOMEONE very similar.

JACK: Someone?

QUINCEY: If blood's what she needs, count me in!

LUCY: *(wakes)* Professor, what did you give me? I want MORE.

(ALL look at LUCY)

JACK: I've got a bad feeling about this!

(ALL exit)

ACT 3 SCENE 4

(LUCY sleeps; ARTHUR, QUINCEY, JACK, and VAN HELSING enter)

ARTHUR: Morning, Lucy!

QUINCEY: Whoa! She looks like a ghost.

(LUCY gets up)

ARTHUR: Darling, you're ill. Get back in bed.

LUCY: Alright, Arthur. Kiss me goodnight?

ARTHUR: It's morning, but -

LUCY: Kiss me!

ARTHUR: Okay!

(LUCY goes for ARTHUR'S neck, VAN HELSING stops her)

VAN HELSING: Not for your life! Keep away!

(JACK and QUINCEY restrain ARTHUR)

ARTHUR: *(to VAN HELSING)* You're a pain in the neck!

VAN HELSING: I saved YOU from one!

LUCY: Van Helsing, my true friend, and his! Guard him, and give me peace!

VAN HELSING: I swear it!

LUCY: *(to ARTHUR)* Goodbye, my love!

(LUCY dies melodramatically, they sob)

JACK: She's gone.

ARTHUR: NO!!!!

QUINCEY: Miss Lucy's bought the farm.

ALL: What?

QUINCEY: It's a Southern thing.

(ARTHUR and QUINCEY exit sobbing)

JACK: I don't understand.

VAN HELSING: Look at her teeth. She was bitten by the vampire. Now, she is Un-Dead, too.

JACK: Lucy has fangs!?

VAN HELSING: Are you convinced now?

JACK: What do we do?

VAN HELSING: *(casually)* We'll cut off her head and fill her mouth with garlic, and drive a stake through her body.

JACK: That's gross!

VAN HELSING: It must be done.

(ALL exit)

ACT 4 SCENE 1

(ARTHUR, QUINCEY, JACK, VAN HELSING enter)

ARTHUR: Why are we visiting Lucy's grave so early?

VAN HELSING: You'll see. Jack, open her coffin.

(Jack "opens" coffin)

QUINCEY: Where's Lucy?

ARTHUR: Someone stole her!

(LUCY enters; ALL scream)

JACK: Lucy?

VAN HELSING: I told you she's undead.

ARTHUR: She's drop undead gorgeous!

LUCY: Leave these others and come to me, Arthur.

VAN HELSING: Get back in your coffin! *(holds up cross, forces Lucy into coffin)* Arthur, am I to proceed?

ARTHUR: *(holds up stake)* I'll do it.

VAN HELSING: Brave lad! This stake must be driven through her heart.

(ARTHUR stabs LUCY, she dies again)

QUINCEY: Now she shall take her place with the other Angels.

JACK: Not yet. You should go, this next part's really gross.

QUINCEY: *(indicates audience)* I don't think they want to see it either.

JACK: Right. *(to VAN HELSING)* Let's do this offstage.

VAN HELSING: *(shrugs)* The CORPSE of true love never did run smooth.

(ALL exit)

ACT 4 SCENE 2

(JONATHAN, MINA, JACK, QUINCEY, VAN HELSING, and ARTHUR enter)

JACK: Welcome to my hospital.

MINA: My new husband and I heard that Dracula killed Lucy. Thank you for letting us stay here while we figure out what to do.

JACK: No one need ever know.

MINA: But they must! In the struggle which we have before us to rid the earth of this terrible monster, we must have all the knowledge.

ARTHUR: We need have no secrets amongst us.

JONATHAN: You should know, Dracula shipped fifty coffins to Carfax Abbey.

JACK: I saw several coffins removed from there last week.

VAN HELSING: That's not good! We must find and destroy all the coffins, then Dracula can't rest in them. He'll be down for the COUNT!

QUINCEY: Ready to hunt vampires?

ALL: 1,2,3 Vampire Hunters! *(ALL high five)*

MINA: Let's do this!

ARTHUR: Wait, you're a lady.

MINA: So?

VAN HELSING: We men are determined to destroy this monster; but it is no part for a woman.

MINA: What?! Who said so?

VAN HELSING: Bram Stoker. Sorry.

JONATHAN: You'll be safer here.

(ALL but MINA exit)

MINA: Fine, but I'm giving Bram a piece of my mind when I see him!!

(RENFIELD enters)

MINA: Oh, hello.

RENFIELD: Hi, I'm Renfield. You're not the girl the doctor wanted to marry.

MINA: I know. I'm Mrs. Harker. My husband and I are visiting Dr. Seward.

RENFIELD: Then don't stay!

MINA: Why not?

RENFIELD: We're all mad here. I've eaten all my pets and tried to kill the doctor because "Blood is life."

MINA: Are you going to hurt me?

RENFIELD: Never!

MINA: Then I hope I may see you often, my friend. Goodnight! *(exits)*

RENFIELD: Good-bye, my dear.

(exits saying "blood is life!")

ACT 4 SCENE 3

(JACK, VAN HELSING, QUINCEY, and ARTHUR enter)

ARTHUR: We've destroyed forty-one coffins. The rest are in Piccadilly.

QUINCEY: That's one busy place. We'll need a plan to sneak in.

VAN HELSING: I have an idea.

(RENFIELD, injured, runs in, screams, and collapses)

QUINCEY: What has happened to him? Poor, poor devil!

RENFIELD: Quick, Doctor, quick. I am dying! I have something that I must say before I die. Dracula offered me power if I'd let him into the hospital. A vampire can't come in unless invited, but once in, he can come and go as he pleases.

JACK: You let Dracula in here?!

RENFIELD: I'm sorry. When Mina came in to see me this afternoon she wasn't the same. All her blood seemed to have run out. It made me mad to know that HE had been taking the life out of her.

ARTHUR: Dracula's been biting MINA? Did he do this to you?

RENFIELD: Yes! I didn't mean Him to take any more of her life. So, I fought him, but Dracula's stronger than me. Please save her! *(dies)*

JACK: Poor fellow, he died trying to protect Mina.

VAN HELSING: We know the worst now. HE is here.

QUINCEY: Dracula could be biting Mina right now! Let's go!

(ALL exit)

ACT 4 SCENE 4

(JONATHAN and MINA; JONATHAN sleeps, DRACULA sneaks up behind MINA)

DRACULA: Come to me, Mina. Please?

MINA: AH! Don't BAT your eyes at me.

DRACULA: Fine. You leave me no choice. *(puts cape around MINA; makes slurping noises)*

MINA: Stop! *(pushes DRACULA away)*

DRACULA: Be my bride. Drink my blood!

MINA: EW!!!

DRACULA: *(hypnotizes MINA)* You will drink.

MINA: I will drink... *(DRACULA conceals MINA in his cape, MINA makes slurping noises)*

(JACK, VAN HELSING, QUINCEY, and ARTHUR enter holding crosses)

JONATHAN: *(wakes)* What!? Oh, do something to save her!

QUINCEY: You better skedaddle, Sucker!

DRACULA: Vampire Hunters! *(exits)*

JONATHAN: Guard her while I look for HIM!

MINA: No! Jonathan, you must not leave me. *(JONATHAN tries to hug her)* No, I'm unclean! Dracula's turning me into a vampire. *(sobs)*

VAN HELSING: No, he's not. I'll prove it. *(holds up a cracker)*

QUINCEY: With a cracker?

VAN HELSING: It's a holy wafer. Holy things burn vampires. *(touches MINA's forehead)*

MINA: *(puts hand to forehead)* AHHH!!! It burns! I'm unclean! Unclean!

JACK: That's gonna leave a mark.

ARTHUR: We must destroy Dracula and the rest of his coffins.

QUINCEY: Don't worry, Mina. We'll keep you from becoming a bloodsucker.

(ALL exit)

ACT 5 SCENE 1

(enter JONATHAN, VAN HELSING, JACK, and MINA with mark on her forehead)

JONATHAN: Mina, Dracula escaped with his last coffin.

VAN HELSING: Things have gone from bat to worse.

MINA: You mean bad?

VAN HELSING: I know what I said.

MINA: Professor, I can read Dracula's thoughts. I think he can read mine, too. Be careful what you say.

JACK: Wow! Just like Harry and Voldemort.

ALL: Who?

JACK: Nevermind.

VAN HELSING: Where's Dracula going?

MINA: He's inside the coffin, on a ship back to Transylvania.

JONATHAN: Let's take the train, we'll beat him there.

VAN HELSING: Time is now to be dreaded—since once he put that mark upon you. We can't stop him without you, Mina.

MINA: Let's hunt some vampires!

(ALL high five and exit)

ACT 5 SCENE 2

(enter VAN HELSING and MINA)

VAN HELSING: There are three ways to reach the castle from here. Since we split up, one group should catch Dracula before he reaches the castle.

MINA: I hope you're right..

VAN HELSING: I hope we're going the right way.

MINA: This is the way.

VAN HELSING: How know you it? *(MINA points to scar)* Right. Let's camp here. Are you hungry?

MINA: No.

VAN HELSING: You haven't eaten all day.

(enter BRIDES)

BRIDES: Hello, Sister.

VAN HELSING: Stay here, Mina. I'll crumble holy wafers around our campfire for safety.

MINA: None safer in all the world from them than I am.

BRIDE 1: Come, Sister.

BRIDE 2: Come to us.

BRIDE 3: You're one of us.

MINA: I can't cross the crumbs.

BRIDES: Soon, you'll be with us forever. *(exit laughing evilly)*

VAN HELSING: Wow. Talk about some weird sisters!

(VAN HELSING and MINA exit)

ACT 5 SCENE 3

(BRIDES enter; sleep; VAN HELSING enters with three stakes)

VAN HELSING: Good. They're sleeping. Then, I will get to my terrible work. Easing it with puns. *(to BRIDE 1)* This is a stake down!

BRIDE 1: *(stands)* I'm not going to stake this lying down! *(he "stakes" her)*

Ohhhh... yes, I am. *(dies melodramatically)*

VAN HELSING: *(to BRIDE 2)* Congratulations! You've won the sweep-stakes!

BRIDE 2: *(sits up)* I didn't' enter any - *(he "stakes" her; she dies)*

VAN HELSING: This is pain-staking! *(to BRIDE 3)* Your turn.

BRIDE 3: *(stands)* Don't go staking my heart!

VAN HELSING: I'll stake your breath away! *("stakes" her; she dies)*

(enter MINA, JACK, and ARTHUR)

ARTHUR: What a mess!

VAN HELSING: I stake no prisoners!

JACK: That's enough, Professor.

VAN HELSING: Sorry! My mi-stake! *(laughing to self)*

(JONATHAN, QUINCEY, and DRACULA enter fighting)

JONATHAN: We've got you now, Sucker!

DRACULA: No way!

VAN HELSING: Quick! Night is coming. He's getting stronger.

(MINA discreetly wipes off her "scar" during the following)

QUINCEY: *(stabs DRACULA's heart)* Another one bites the dust!

JONATHAN: *(stabs DRACULA)* This is for Mina!

DRACULA: That's the final nail in my coffin! *(dies)*

VAN HELSING: Mina, your scar is gone! The curse has passed away!

QUINCEY: She's saved! *(groans; holds side)*

ARTHUR: Quincey, you've been stabbed!

QUINCEY: It's just a flesh wound. I'll walk it off. *(staggers)*

JACK: I don't think so.

QUINCEY: I am only too happy to have been of any service! It was worth for this to die! *(dies)*

JONATHAN: We'll never forget you!

MINA: We'll name our firstborn Quincey.

QUINCEY: *(leans up)* Yee-haw! *(dies again)*

VAN HELSING: *(to Mina)* Someday your son will read about what a brave and gallant woman his mother is.

JACK: Good has triumphed over evil.

ALL: 1,2,3, Vampire Hunters!

(ALL high five; exit)

(NARRATOR enters)

NARRATOR: Was that punny or what?! Bummer about Quincy, though. But hey, what's a cowboy doing in a Dracula show, anyway? I mean, what was Stoker thinking? "I know what it would really make this work, a cowboy!" But, seriously folks, we did it. We got rid of all the monsters. None of you died. Right? You're all here? Good. Most importantly, I didn't die. Now let's thank this marvelous cast for all their great work!

(cast calls)

NARRATOR: *(to audience)* Thank you, everyone, and...

ALL: Goodnight!

(MONSTERS sneak forward, grab NARRATOR, and take him offstage)

NARRATOR: Nooooooo.....

ABOUT THE AUTHORS

ANGELA M. HERRICK is a drama teacher, actor, writer, and director and has a passion for storytelling. A teacher at heart, she believes in retelling these classic stories in a way that makes them fun and accessible for the next generation. Angela lives on the Central Coast of California and loves hanging out with her husband, five children, Savannah the dog, and cats Gatsby and Mayhem.

AMANDA THAYER loves books more than most things (excepting maybe her husband and children). She has a B.A. in English and a Master of Library Studies from the University of North Carolina at Greensboro. She is also an actress and dramaturg, having worked with SLO Repertory Theatre, The Great American Melodrama, and PCPA. Amanda grew up performing and understands the importance of youth arts programs. Amanda likes to laugh and she hopes you do too!

BRENDAN P. KELSO came to writing modified Shakespeare scripts when he was taking time off from work to be at home with his newly born son. "It just grew from there". Within months, he was being asked to offer classes in various locations and acting organizations along the Central Coast of California. Originally employed as an engineer, Brendan never thought about writing. However, his unique personality, humor, and love for engaging kids with The Bard has led him to leave the engineering world and pursue writing as a new adventure in life! He has always believed, "the best way to learn is to have fun!" Brendan makes his home on the Central Coast of California and loves to spend time with his wife and kids.

CAST AUTOGRAPHS

www.ingramcontent.com/pod-product-compliance
Lightning Source LLC
Chambersburg PA
CBHW050654160426
43194CB00010B/1937